NOTHING
PERSONAL

SELECTED WORKS
by James Baldwin

■ ESSAYS AND POETRY ■

Notes of a Native Son (1955)
Nobody Knows My Name: More Notes of a Native Son (1961)
The Fire Next Time (1963)
No Name in the Street (1972)
Jimmy's Blues (1983)
The Evidence of Things Not Seen (1985)
The Price of the Ticket (1985)
Jimmy Blues and Other Poems (2014)

■ NOVELS AND STORIES ■

Go Tell It on the Mountain (1953)
Giovanni's Room (1956)
Another Country (1962)
Going to Meet the Man (1965)
Tell Me How Long the Train's Been Gone (1968)
If Beale Street Could Talk (1974)
Just Above My Head (1979)

NOTHING PERSONAL

JAMES BALDWIN

BEACON PRESS
BOSTON

BEACON PRESS
Boston, Massachusetts
www.beacon.org

Beacon Press books
are published under the auspices of
the Unitarian Universalist Association of Congregations.

24 23   8 7 6 5 4

This book is printed on acid-free paper that meets
the uncoated paper ANSI/NISO specifications
for permanence as revised in 1992.

Text design and composition by Kim Arney

Library of Congress Cataloging-in-Publication Data
is available for this title.

CONTENTS

FOREWORD

IN 1964, James Baldwin and Richard Avedon collaborated on *Nothing Personal*. The images were by Avedon; words by Baldwin. They'd known each other for decades by then, having worked together on *The Magpie* literary magazine at DeWitt Clinton High School in the Bronx, as teens. In the intervening years, each had achieved success as artists and cultural documentarians. They shared a gift for depth and the ability to capture the zeitgeist. The interplay of words and images in the original version of the book offer an intriguing historical account of mid-twentieth-century American culture.

Here Baldwin's essay stands alone. Something dramatic results. The work transforms from artifact to a breathtaking and prophetic witness. In reading it, I was dumbstruck. How, I wondered, could Baldwin have known what the information age, social media, and the marketization of everything—a shorthand for our current state of late capitalist living— would do to us? How did he know how it would shape us?

Baldwin's alchemy was a result of his habit of careful observation and deep study. He watched television. It is a mirror. Then, and now: we have acquired an endless habit of the most superficial forms of self-correction, makeup to make up for our perceived inadequacy as it were, nipping, tucking, coloring, all as a displacement for the possibilities of deeper self-reflection and self-creation. Our consumptiveness, Baldwin argues, is so pervasive that sex has become commodity rather than intimacy. If we didn't know these words were published in 1964, we might assume that they describe the social media, one-click buying and marketing, the pornographic algorithms of desire, our cyborg selves (part screen, part machine, and a little bit of human) and the simulacra which inundate us in the 2020s. Simply put, he saw the twenty-first century in the middle of the twentieth.

With that kind of prophetic fire, of course, we have to take his indictments of our society seriously. Recognizing that Americans live as terrified adolescents, he argues:

> This terror has something to do with that irreducible gap between the self one invents—the self one takes oneself as being, which is, however and by definition, a provisional self—and the undiscoverable self which always has the power to blow the provisional self to bits. It is perfectly possible—indeed, it is far from uncommon—to go to bed one night, or wake up one morning, or simply walk through a door one has known all one's life, and discover, between inhaling and exhaling,

that the self one has sewn together with such effort is all dirty rags, is unusable, is gone: and out of what raw material will one build a self again?

This fear, he claims, reaches all the way to the top. And in that assessment, Baldwin even anticipates the age of Trump. The male politician who, as he describes it, is "absolutely indistinguishable from the American boy. He doesn't even seem much closer to the grave—which fact, in the case of most of our most influential politicians, fills a great many people, all over the world, with despair." And that perhaps is the heart of the lesson. Captured in an unrepentant childlike state we are too eager to think we can just turn a page or turn a blind eye. We want to escape the ugliest of moments and are therefore bound to repeat them.

So to repeat his question: How will we build a self, again?

Certainly these pages offer a guide. By holding fast to American mythologies, we endanger justice, and we engender injustice. Baldwin describes the "inert" Plymouth Rock as a gravestone for Indians, Africans, and the potential of white Americans' humanity. That rock, a literal historic artifact and a national narrative, is a death knell for the truth. The truth, as Baldwin sees it, is that "the country was settled by a desperate, divided, and rapacious horde of people who were determined to forget their pasts and determined to make money."

As long as Americans, and in particular white Americans, hold fast to the myth and remain stuck in the idolatries of the past, they deprive themselves of a usable past, one from which to learn. For Baldwin, this is something more than what Marx described as false consciousness. It is both shaped circumstance and deliberate choice, and it is as personal as it is political. We do not have to be this way.

As we read his words today, I hope, we can honor the indictment and consider our choices. What, for example, is the usable but neglected past at our disposal? It isn't only found in the mythic origins but even in how we describe many of our most heroic historic events. For example, we find ourselves subject to a conventional narrative of civil rights that leads us to a tidy conclusion. See! It says, We made mistakes, but we have taken strides steadily to an ever more perfect union. Baldwin decried that mythology even as it was being created. The last two decades of his life, he wrangled with those fictions and fantasies as Eddie Glaude so brilliantly and unflinchingly captures in his book *Begin Again*. Indeed, racial inequality persists and has been extended in the intervening decades. Even more ironic perhaps, many public and powerful figures cite Baldwin as a hero today, while evading the fact that those who take up the courage of conviction in precisely the way Baldwin once did are often avoided *assiduously* or punished for speaking truth to power. I hope that Baldwin's words here remind you that, notwithstanding the way the world has changed when it comes to race since 1964, despite all the elected officials, all the celebrities, all the celebrated "firsts," we have not been able to escape its ugly grasp.

In this piece you will read Baldwin's description of an experience he had with a Swiss friend. They're arrested and separated. He's accustomed to such abuses as a Black American man. Harassment, targeting, unlawful arrest. But he worries about his friend. His friend, he learns later, is warned while in custody against befriending "niggers" if he is to make his way in the United States. And in his own experience, Baldwin recognizes a familiar disappointment in the cop who wishes Baldwin had committed *any* infraction. It would have been not only a justification for the arrest but a legitimation of the racist practices of policing.

The casual racism, the disciplining voice of white supremacy, and, of course, the actions of police themselves are all resonant today. In fact, if one were to do an overview of Black politically informed writing from the beginning of the twentieth century to the end, the police are a recurring theme. As an arm of state power, as a tool of state violence, the institution has long been a knife in the side of Black America. That we act as though the Movement for Black Lives has newly raised this issue is not a sign of its novelty. Nor is it a sign that we simply needed proof in camera phones. The fact that we treat this issue as new is the *evidence* that we have failed our history, as Baldwin charges. And at the same time, what Baldwin calls the "discovery" and "invention" (and they are often the same) of the "barbarian" continues. That term as he used it, is sarcastic of course. Threatening "others" is a recurring and recycled trope in the American imagination. Even today, the Cold War, long over, gets re-triggered in panics over "socialism." Nativism is regurgitated in narratives of Central American intrusion, and xenophobia is ignited in terrorizing caricatures of the Middle East. And of course, the words "thug," "urban," and "welfare" dredge up centuries old US anti-Blackness. Being stuck in the past is, we see, a creative venture. It is the matter of same roles but new demons. But, and this is Baldwin's hope for us, if we allow ourselves a history, we might see our way to something good.

Considering myself his pupil in the study of humanity, and an emulator when it comes to his methods, I've tried to take up a habit he describes here. Baldwin walked through city streets looking at people. I'm doing the same these days. I'm writing in the time of COVID, a season during which most of us are wearing masks. As a result, with only glimpses at flared nostrils or fake smiles, our eyes are even more exposed. They are, as Baldwin told me to expect, exhausted and terrified. They scan and they disappear into worry. They are also more luminous in their nakedness. My overview of the public is limited, though. Fewer people are out these days, because public spaces pose an immediate danger. We are sequestered. And it is easy to navel gaze, to see our adversity, terror, exhaustion, and worry as private suffering. But as Baldwin once said, reading allows us to recognize each other. It is nothing personal. It makes everything seem possible. May we find hope in his brilliant words.

—Imani Perry

NOTHING
PERSONAL

ONE

I USED TO DISTRACT MYSELF, some mornings before I got out of bed, by pressing the television remote control gadget from one channel to another. This may be the only way to watch TV: I certainly saw some remarkable sights. Blondes and brunettes and, possibly, redheads—my screen was colorless—washing their hair, relentlessly smiling, teeth gleaming like the grillwork of automobiles, breasts firmly, chillingly encased—packaged, as it were—and brilliantly uplifted, forever, all sagging corrected, forever, all middle age bulge—*defeated,* eyes as sensuous and mysterious as jelly beans, lips covered with cellophane, hair sprayed to the consistency of aluminum, girdles forbidden to slide up, stockings defeated in their subversive tendencies to slide down, to tum crooked, to snag, to run, to tear, hands prevented from aging by incredibly soft detergents, fingernails forbidden to break by superbly smooth enamels, teeth forbidden to decay by mysterious chemical formulas, all conceivable body odor, under no matter what contingency, prevented for twenty-four hours of every day, forever and forever and forever, children's bones knit strong by the foresight of vast bakeries, tobacco robbed of any harmful effects by the addition of mint, the removal of nicotine, the presence of filters and the length of the cigarette, tires which cannot betray you, automobiles which will make you feel proud, doors which cannot slam on those precious fingers or fingernails, diagrams illustrating—proving—how swiftly impertinent pain can be driven away, square-jawed youngsters danc-ing, other square-jawed youngsters, armed with guitars, or backed by bands, howling; all of this—and so much more—punctuated by the roar of great automobiles, overtaking gangsters, the spatter of tommy-guns mow-ing them down, the rise of the organ as the Heroine braces herself to Tell All, the moving smile of the housewife who has just won a fortune in metal and crockery; news—news?

from where?—dropping into this sea with the alertness and irrelevancy of pebbles, sex wearing an aspect so implacably dispiriting that even masturbation (by no means mutual) seems one of the possibilities that vanished in Eden, and murder one's last, best hope—sex of an appalling coyness, often in the form of a prophylactic cigarette being extended by the virile male toward the aluminum and cellophane girl. They happily blow smoke into each other's face, jelly beans, brilliant with desire, grillwork gleaming; perhaps—poor, betrayed exiles—they are trying to discover if, behind all that grillwork, all those barriers, either of them has a tongue.

Subsequently, in the longer and less explicit commercials in which these images are encased, the male certainly doesn't seem to have a tongue—perhaps one may say that the cat's got it; father knows best, these days, only in politics, which is the only place we ever find him, and where he proves to be—alas!—absolutely indistinguishable from the American boy. He doesn't even seem much closer to the grave—which fact, in the case of most of our most influential politicians, fills a great many people, all over the world, with despair.

And so it should. We have all heard the bit about what a pity it was that Plymouth Rock didn't land on the Pilgrims instead of the other way around. I have never found this remark very funny. It seems wistful and vindictive to me, containing, furthermore, a very bitter truth. The inertness of that rock meant death for the Indians, enslavement for the blacks, and spiritual disaster for those homeless Europeans who now call themselves Americans and who have never been able to resolve their relationship either to the continent they fled or to the continent they conquered. Leaving aside—as we, mostly, imagine ourselves to be able to do—those people to whom we quaintly refer as minorities, who, without the most tremendous coercion, coercion indistinguishable from despair, would ever have crossed the frightening ocean to come to this desolate place? I know the myth tells us that heroes came, looking for freedom; just as the myth tells us that America is full of smiling people. Well, heroes are always, by definition, looking for freedom, and no doubt a few heroes got here, too—one wonders how they fared; and though I rarely see anyone smiling here, I am prepared to believe that many people are, though God knows what it is they're smiling about; but the relevant truth is that the country was settled by a desperate, divided, and rapacious horde of people who were determined to forget their pasts and determined to make money. We certainly have not changed in this respect and this is proved by our faces, by our children, by our absolutely unspeakable loneliness, and the spectacular ugliness and hostility of our cities. Our cities are terribly unloved—by the people who live in them, I mean. No one seems to feel that the city belongs to him.

Despair: perhaps it is this despair which we should attempt to examine if we hope to bring water to this desert.

It is, of course, in the very nature of a myth that those who are its victims and, at the same time, its perpetrators, should, by virtue of these two facts, be rendered unable to examine the myth, or even to suspect, much less recognize, that it is a myth which controls and blasts their lives. One sees this, it seems to me, in great and grim relief, in the situation of the poor white in the Deep South. The poor white was enslaved almost from the instant he arrived on these shores, and he is still enslaved by a brutal and cynical oligarchy. The utility of the poor white was to make slavery both profitable and safe

and, therefore, the germ of white supremacy which he brought with him from Europe
was made hideously to flourish in the American air. Two world wars and a world-wide
depression have failed to reveal to this poor
man that he has far more in common with the
ex-slaves whom he fears than he has with the
masters who oppress them both for profit.
It is no accident that ancient Scottish ballads
and Elizabethan chants are still heard in those
dark hills—talk about a people being locked
in the past! To be locked in the past means,
in effect, that one has no past, since one can
never assess it, or use it: and if one cannot use
the past, one cannot function in the present,
and so one can never be free. I take this to be,
as I say, the American situation in relief, the

root of our unadmitted sorrow, and the very key to our crisis.

It has always been much easier (because it has always seemed much safer) to give a name to the evil without than to locate the terror within. And yet, the terror within is far truer and far more powerful than any of our labels: the labels change, the terror is constant. And this terror has something to do with that irreducible gap between the self one invents—the self one takes oneself as being, which is, however and by definition , a provisional self—and the undiscoverable self which always has the power to blow the provisional self to bits. It is perfectly possible—indeed, it is far from uncommon—to go to bed one night, or wake up one morning, or simply walk through a door

one has known all one's life, and discover, between inhaling and exhaling, that the self one
has sewn together with such effort is all dirty
rags, is unusable, is gone: and out of what
raw material will one build a self again? The
lives of men—and, therefore, of nations—to
an extent literally unimaginable, depend on
how vividly this question lives in the mind. It
is a question which can paralyze the mind, of
course; but if the question does *not* live in the
mind, then one is simply condemned to eternal youth, which is a synonym for corruption.

Some rare days, often in the winter, when
New York is cheerfully immobilized by snow—
cheerfully, because the snow gives people an
excuse to talk to each other, and they need,
God help us, an excuse—or sometimes when

the frozen New York spring is approaching, I walk out of my house toward no particular destination, and watch the faces that pass me. Where do they come from? how did they become—these faces—so cruel and so sterile? they are related to whom? they are related to what? They do not relate to the buildings, certainly—no human being could; I suspect, in fact, that many of us live with the carefully suppressed terror that these buildings are about to crash down on us; the nature of the movement of the people in the streets is certainly very close to panic. You will search in vain for lovers. I have not heard anyone singing in the streets of New York for more than twenty years. By singing, I mean singing for joy, for the hell of it. I don't mean the drunken, lonely,

4-AM keening which is simply the sound of some poor soul trying to vomit up his anguish and gagging on it. Where the people can sing, the poet can live—and it is worth saying it the other way around, too: where the poet can sing, the people can live. When a civilization treats its poets with the disdain with which we treat ours, it cannot be far from disaster; it cannot be far from the slaughter of the innocents. Everyone is rushing, God knows where, and everyone is looking for God knows what—but it is clear that no one is happy here, and that something has been lost. Only, sometimes, uptown, along the river, perhaps, I've sometimes watched strangers here, here for a day or a week or a month, or newly transplanted, watched a boy and a girl, or a boy and a boy, or a man and a woman, or a man and a child, or a woman and a child; yes, *there* was something recognizable, something to which the soul responded, something to make one smile, even to make one weep with exultation. They were yet distinguishable from the concrete and the steel. One felt that one might approach them without freezing to death.

TWO

A EUROPEAN FRIEND of mine and myself were arrested on Broadway, in broad day-light, while looking for a taxi. He had been here three days, had not yet mastered English, and I was showing him the wonders of the city of New York. He was impressed and bewildered, though he also seemed rather to wonder what purpose it served—when, suddenly, down from heaven, or up through the sidewalk, two plain-clothes men appeared, separated us, scarcely a word was spoken. I watched my friend, carried by the scruff of the neck, vanish into the crowd. Not a soul seemed to notice; apparently it happened every day. I was pushed into the doorway of a drugstore, and frisked, made to empty my pockets, made to roll up my sleeves, asked what I was doing around here—"around here" being the city in which I was born.

I am an old hand at this—policemen have always loved to pick me up and, sometimes, to beat me up—so I said nothing during this entire operation. I was worried about my friend, who might fail to understand the warmth of his reception in the land of the free; worried about his command of English, especially

when confronted by the somewhat special
brand used by the police. Neither of us carried knives or guns, neither of us used dope:
so much for the criminal aspect. Furthermore,
my friend was a married man, with two children, here on a perfectly respectable visit, and
he had not even come from some dirty and
disreputable place, like Greece, but from geo-
metric and solvent Switzerland: so much for
morals. I was not exactly a bum, either, so I
wondered what the cop would say.

He seemed extremely disappointed that
I carried no weapons, that my veins were
not punctured—disappointed, and, therefore, more truculent than ever. I conveyed to
him with some force that I was not precisely

helpless and that I was perfectly able, and more than willing, to cause him a great deal of trouble. Why, exactly, had he picked us up?

He was now confused, afraid, and apologetic, which caused me to despise him from the bottom of my heart. He said—how many times have I heard it!—that there had been a call out to pick up two guys who looked just like us.

White and black, you mean?

Apart from my friends, I think I can name on the fingers of one hand all the Americans I have ever met who were able to answer a direct question, a real question: well, not exactly. Hell, no. He hadn't even known that the other guy was white. (He thought that he was Puerto Rican, which says something very interesting, I think, about the eye of the be-holder—like, as it were, to like.)

Nevertheless, he was in a box—it was not going to be a simple matter of apologizing and letting me go. Unless he was able to find his friend and *my* friend, I was going to force him to arrest me and then bring charges for false arrest. So, not without difficulty, we found my friend, who had been released and was waiting in the bar around the corner from our house. He, also, had baffled his interlocutor; had baffled him by turning out to be exactly what he had said he was, which contains its own com-ment, I think, concerning the attitudes Ameri-cans have toward each other. He had given my friend a helpful tip: if he wanted to make it in America, it would be better for him not to be seen with niggers. My friend thanked him warmly, which brought a glow, I should imagine, to his simple heart—how we adore simplicity!—and has since made something of a point of avoiding white Americans.

I certainly can't blame him. For one thing, talking to Americans is usually extremely uphill work. We are afraid to reveal ourselves because we trust ourselves so little. American attitudes are appalling, but so are the attitudes of most of the people in the world. What is stultifying here is that the attitude is presented as the person; one is expected to justify the attitude in order to reassure the person— whom, alas, one has yet to meet, who is light-years away, in some dreadful, private labyrinth. And in this labyrinth the person is desperately trying *not* to find out what he *really* feels. Therefore, the truth cannot be told, even about one's attitudes: we live by lies. And not only, for example, about race— whatever, by this time, in this country, or, in- deed, in the world, this word may mean—but about our very natures. The lie has penetrated to our most private moments, and the most secret chambers of our hearts.

Nothing more sinister can happen, in any society, to any people. And when it happens, it means that the people are caught in a kind of vacuum between their present and their past— the romanticized, that is, the maligned past, and the denied and dishonored present. It is a crisis of identity. And in such a crisis, at such a pressure, it becomes absolutely indispensable to discover, or invent—the two words, here, are synonyms—the stranger, the barbarian, who is responsible for our confusion and our pain. Once he is driven out—destroyed— then we can be at peace: those questions will be gone. Of course, those questions never go, but it has always seemed much easier to murder than to change. And this is really the choice with which we are confronted now.

I know that these are strong words for a sunlit, optimistic land, lulled for so long, and into such an euphoria, by prosperity (based on the threat of war) and by such magazines as *Reader's Digest,* and stirring political slogans, and Hollywood and television. (Communications whose role is not to communicate, but simply to reassure.) Nevertheless, I am appalled—for example—by the limpness with which the entire nation appears to have accepted the proposition that, in the city of Dallas, Texas, in which handbills were being issued accusing the late President Kennedy of treason, one would *need* a leftist lunatic with a gun to blow off the President's head. Leftists have a hard time in the south; there cannot be very many there; I, certainly, was never followed around southern streets by leftist lunatics, but state troopers. Similarly, there are a great many people in Texas, or, for that matter, in America, with far stronger reasons for wishing the President dead than any demented Castroite could have had. Quite apart, now, from what time will reveal the truth of this case to have been, it is reassuring to feel that the evil came from without and is in no way connected with the moral climate of America; reassuring to feel that the enemy sent the assassin from far away, and that we, ourselves, could never have nourished so monstrous a personality or be in any way whatever responsible for such a cowardly and bloody act. Well. The America of my experience has worshipped and nourished violence for as long as I have been on earth. The violence was being perpetrated mainly against black men, though—the strangers; and so it didn't count. But, if a society permits one portion of its citizenry to be menaced or destroyed, then, very soon, no one in that society is safe. The forces thus released in the people can never be held in check, but run their devouring course, destroying the very foundations which it was imagined they would save.

But we are unbelievably ignorant concerning what goes on in our country—to say nothing of what goes on in the rest of the world—and appear to have become too timid to question what we are told. Our failure to trust one another deeply enough to be able to talk to one another has become so great that people with these questions in their hearts do not speak them; our opulence is so pervasive that people who are afraid to lose whatever they think they have persuade themselves of the truth of a lie, and help disseminate it; and God help the innocent here, that man or woman who simply wants to love, and be loved.

Unless this would-be lover is able to replace his or her backbone with a steel rod, he or she is doomed. This is no place for love. I know that I am now expected to make a bow in the direction of those millions of unremarked, happy marriages all over America, but I am unable honestly to do so because I find nothing whatever in our moral and social climate—and I am now thinking particularly of the state of our children—to bear witness to their existence. I suspect that when we refer to these happy and so marvelously invisible people, we are simply being nostalgic concerning the happy, simple, God-fearing life which we imagine ourselves once to have lived. In any case, wherever love is found, it unfailingly makes itself felt in the individual, the personal

authority of the individual. Judged by this
standard, we are a loveless nation. The best
that can be said is that some of us are struggling. And what we are struggling against is
that death in the heart which leads not only
to the shedding of blood, but which reduces
human beings to corpses while they live.

THREE

FOUR AM can be a devastating hour. The day, no matter what kind of day it was, is indisputably over; almost instantaneously, a new day begins: and how will one bear it? Probably no better than one bore the day that is ending, possibly not as well. Moreover, a day is coming which one will not recall, that last day of one's life, and on that day one will *oneself* become as irrecoverable as all the days that have passed.

It is a fearful speculation—or, rather, a fearful knowledge—that, one day one's eyes will no longer look out on the world. One will no longer be present at the universal morning roll call. The light will rise for others, but not for you. Sometimes, at four AM, this knowledge is almost enough to force a reconciliation between oneself and all one's pain and error. Since, anyway, it will end one day, why not try it—life—one more time? *It's a long old road,* as Bessie Smith puts it, *but it's got to find an end.* And so, she wearily, doggedly, informs us, *I picked up my bag, baby, and I tried it again.* Her song ends on a very bitter and revealing note: *You can't trust nobody, you might as well be alone / found my long-lost friend, and I might as well stayed at home!*

Still, she was driven to find that long-lost friend, to grasp again, with fearful hope, the unwilling, unloving, human hand. I think all of our voyages drive us there; for I have always felt that a human being could only be saved by another human being. I am aware that we do not save each other very often. But I am also aware that we save each other some of the time. And all that God can do, and all that I expect Him to do, is lend one the courage to continue one's journey and face one's end, when it comes, like a man.

For, perhaps—perhaps—between now and that last day, something wonderful will happen, a miracle, a miracle of coherence and release. And the miracle on which one's unsteady attention is focussed is always the same, however it may be stated, or however it may remain unstated. It is the miracle of love, love strong enough to guide or drive one into the great estate of maturity, or, to put it another way, into the apprehension and acceptance of one's own identity. For some deep and ineradicable instinct—I believe—causes us to know that it is only this passionate achievement which can outlast death, which can cause life to spring from death.

Nevertheless, sometimes, at four AM, when one feels that one has probably become simply incapable of supporting this miracle, with all one's wounds awake and throbbing, and all one's ghastly inadequacy staring and shouting from the walls and the floor—the entire universe having shrunk to the prison of the self—death glows like the only light on a high, dark, mountain road, where one has, forever and forever! lost one's way. And many of us perish then.

But if one can reach back, reach down— into oneself, into one's life—and find there some witness, however unexpected or am- bivalent, to one's reality, one will be enabled, though perhaps not very spiritedly, to face an- other day. (We used to sing in the church, *It's another day's journey, and I'm so glad, the world can't do me no harm!*) What one must be enabled to recognize, at four o'clock in the morning, is that one has no right, at least not for reasons of private anguish, to take one's life. All lives are connected to other lives and when one man goes, much more than the man goes with him.

One has to look on oneself as the custodian of a quantity and a quality—oneself—which is absolutely unique in the world because it has never been here before and will never be here again. But it is extremely difficult, in this place and time, to look on oneself in this way. Where all human connections are distrusted, the human being is very quickly lost.

Four AM passes, the dangerous turning maneuvered once more; and here comes the sun or the rain and the hard, metallic, unrevealing light and sounds of life outside and movement in the streets. Cautiously, one peeks through the blinds, guessing at the weather. And, presently, out of the limbo of the bathroom steam and fog, one's face comes floating up again, from unimaginable depths.

Here it comes, unreadable as ever, the patient bones steady beneath the skin, eyes veiling the mind's bewilderment and the heart's loss, only the lips cryptically suggesting that all is not well with the spirit which lives within this clay. Then one selects the uniform which one will wear. This uniform is designed to tele-graph to others what to see so that they will not be made uncomfortable and probably hos-tile by being forced to look on another human being. The uniform must suggest a certain setting and it must dictate a certain air and it must also convey, however subtly, a dormant aggressiveness, like the power of a sleeping lion. It is necessary to make anyone on the streets think twice before attempting to vent his despair on you. So armed, one reaches the unloved streets. The unloved streets. I have very often walked through the streets of New York fancying myself a kind of unprecedented explorer, trapped among savages, searching for hidden treasure; the trick being to discover the treasure before the savages discovered me; hence, my misleading uniform. After all, I have lived in cities in which stone urns on park parapets were not unthinkable, cities in which it was perfectly possible, and not a matter of taking one's life in one's hands, to walk through the park. How long would a stone urn last in Central Park? And look at the New York buildings, rising up like tyrannical eagles, glass and steel and aluminum smiting the air, jerry-built, inept, contemptuous; who can function in these buildings and for whose profit were they built? Unloved indeed: look at our children. They roam the streets, as arrogant and irreverent as business-men and as dangerous as those gangs of children who roamed the streets of bombed European cities after the last World War. Only, these children have no strange and grinning soldiers to give them chocolate candy or chewing gum, and no one will give them a home. No one has one to give, the very word no longer conveying any meaning, and, anyway, nothing is more vivid in American life than the fact that we have no respect for our children, nor have our children any respect for us. By being what we have become, by placing things above people, we broke their hearts early, and drove them away.

We have, as it seems to me, a very curious sense of reality—or, rather, perhaps, I should say, a striking addiction to irreality. How is it possible, one cannot but ask, to raise a child without loving the child? How is it possible to love the child if one does not know who one is? How is it possible for the child to grow up if the child is not loved? Children can survive without money or security or safety or things: but they are lost if they cannot find a loving example, for only this example can give them a touchstone for their lives. *Thus far and no further*: this is what the father must say to the child. If the child is not told where the limits are, he will spend the rest of his life trying to discover them. For the child who is not told where the limits are knows, though he may not know he knows it, that no one cares enough about him to prepare him for his journey.

This, I think, has something to do with the phenomenon, unprecedented in the world, of the ageless American boy; it has something to do with our desperate adulation of simplicity and youth—how bitterly betrayed one must have been in one's youth to suppose that it is a virtue to remain simple or to remain young!—and it also helps to explicate, to my mind at least, some of the stunning purposes to which Americans have put the imprecise science of psychiatry. I have known people in genuine trouble, who somehow managed to live with their trouble; and I cannot but compare these people—ex-junkies and jail-birds, sons of German Nazis, sons of Spanish

generals, sons of Southern racists, blues sing-
ers and black matrons—with that fluid horde,
in my professional and quasi-professional con-
tacts, whose only real trouble is inertia, who
work at the most disgraceful jobs in order to
pay, for the luxury of someone else's attention, twenty-five dollars an hour. To my black
and toughened, Puritan conscience, it seems
an absolute scandal; and, again, this peculiar
self-indulgence certainly has a dreadful effect
on their children, whom they are quite unable
to raise. And they cannot raise them because
they have opted for the one commodity which
is absolutely beyond human reach: safety.

This is one of the reasons, as it seems
to me, that we are so badly educated, for to
become educated (as all tyrants have always

known) is to become inaccessibly independent, it is to acquire a dangerous way of assessing danger, and it is to hold in one's hands a means of changing reality. This is not at all the same thing as "adjusting" to reality: the effort of "adjusting" to reality simply has the paradoxical effect of destroying reality, since it substitutes for one's own speech and one's own voice an interiorized public cacophony of quotations.

People are defeated or go mad or die in many, many ways, some in the silence of that valley, *where I couldn't hear nobody pray,* and many in the public, sounding horror where no cry or lament or song or hope can disentangle itself from the roar. And so we go under, victims of that universal cruelty which lives in the heart and in the world, victims of the universal indifference to the fate of another, victims of the universal fear of love, proof of the absolute impossibility of achieving a life without love. One day, perhaps, unimaginable generations hence, we will evolve into the knowledge that human beings are more important than real estate and will permit this knowledge to become the ruling principle of our lives. For I do not for an instant doubt, and I will go to my grave believing, that we can build Jerusalem, if we will.

FOUR

*T*HE *LIGHT that's in your eyes / reminds me of the skies / that shine above us every day—* so wrote a contemporary lover, out of God knows what agony, what hope, and what despair. But he saw the light in the eyes, which is the only light there is in the world, and honored it and trusted it; and will always be able to find it; since it is always there, waiting to be found. One discovers the light in darkness, that is what darkness is for; but everything in our lives depends on how we bear the light. It is necessary, while in darkness, to know that there is a light somewhere, to know that in oneself, waiting to be found, there is a light. What the light reveals is danger, and what it demands is faith. Pretend, for example, that you were born in Chicago and have never had the remotest desire to visit Hong Kong, which is only a name on a map for you; pretend that some convulsion, sometimes called accident, throws you into connection with a man or a woman who lives in Hong Kong; and that you fall in love. Hong Kong will immediately cease to be a name and become the center of your life. And you may never know how many people live in Hong Kong. But you will know that one man or one woman lives there without whom you cannot live. And this is how our lives are changed, and this is how we are redeemed.

What a journey this life is! Dependent, entirely, on things unseen. If your lover lives in Hong Kong and cannot get to Chicago, it will be necessary for you to go to Hong Kong. Perhaps you will spend your life there, and never see Chicago again. And you will, I assure you, as long as space and time divide you from anyone you love, discover a great deal about shipping routes, airlines, earth quake, famine, disease, and war. And you will always know what time it is in Hong Kong, for you love someone who lives there. And love will simply have no choice but to go into battle with space and time and, furthermore, to win.

I know we often lose, and that the death or destruction of another is infinitely more real and unbearable than one's own. I think I know how many times one has to start again, and how often one feels that one cannot start again. And yet, on pain of death, one can never remain where one is. The light. The light. One will perish without the light.

I have slept on rooftops and in basements and subways, have been cold and hungry all my life; have felt that no fire would ever warm me, and no arms would ever hold me. I have been, as the song says, *'buked and scorned* and I know that I always will be. But, my God, in that darkness, which was the lot of my ancestors and my own state, what a mighty fire burned! In that darkness of rape and degradation, that fine flying froth and mist of blood, through all that terror and in all that helplessness, a living soul moved and refused to die. We really emptied oceans with a home-made spoon and tore down mountains with our hands. And if love was in Hong Kong, we learned how to swim.

It is a mighty heritage, it is the human heritage, and it is all there is to trust. And I learned this through descending, as it were, into the eyes of my father and my mother. I wondered, when I was little, how they bore it—for I knew that they had much to bear. It had not yet occurred to me that I also would have much to bear; but they knew it, and the unimaginable rigors of their journey helped them to prepare me for mine. This is why one must say *Yes* to life and embrace it wherever it is found—and it is found in terrible places; nevertheless, there it is; and if the father can say, *Yes, Lord,* the child can learn that most difficult of words, *Amen.*

For nothing is fixed, forever and forever and forever, it is not fixed; the earth is always shifting, the light is always changing, the sea does not cease to grind down rock. Generations do not cease to be born, and we are responsible to them because we are the only witnesses they have.

The sea rises, the light fails, lovers cling to each other, and children cling to us. The moment we cease to hold each other, the moment we break faith with one another, the sea engulfs us and the light goes out.

AFTERWORD

NOTHING PERSONAL is an extraordinary piece of writing—perhaps one of James Baldwin's most complex essays. In a moment of profound transition in his life as a "witness" and within the compact space of four relatively brief sections, Baldwin lays bare many of the central themes of his corpus. He writes about history, identity, death, and loneliness. The reader gets a sense of the depth of his despair and his desperate hold on to the power of love in what is, by any measure, a loveless world—especially in a country so obsessed with money. In a sense, *Nothing Personal* sits at the crossroads of his work. *The Fire Next Time* solidified his fame and status as one of America's most insightful writers about race and democracy, but the brutal reality of the black freedom struggle—the murder of Medgar Evers, for example, and the terror of Southern sheriffs—forced him to confront, again, the country's ongoing betrayal. Baldwin, like a conductor approaching a railway switch, signals with this essay the beginning of a shift in tone. Darkness hovers over the writing. One feels his vulnerability on the page.

I must confess that I have rarely lingered here before. I have always read *Nothing Personal* in relation to Richard Avedon's photographs: as if the words only offered an interpretation of what I was seeing. Baldwin's prose was my crutch, because I don't think I am very good at "seeing" such things. So, I skipped the essay when it was included in the collection *The Price of the Ticket*; I preferred reading it alongside the images. But in doing so, I missed something essential: that *Nothing Personal* was, in its own way, an existential coda for the nation (a fugitive thought, perhaps, in a time when one has to steal moments to think). Baldwin wanted us to confront the loveless character of our lives, the prison of our myths, and the illusion of what we take to be "safety." Avedon's images themselves broke up the writing and fragmented the argument about who we are

as a nation and, in doing so, somewhat ob-
scured the claim about the perils of American
adolescence. I was so focused on the images
I couldn't see the sophisticated stitching of
Baldwin's plea. And, my God, in the aftermath
of Donald Trump's presidency, we need to
hear that plea clearly in all of its complexity.

In all of these years of reading Baldwin,
I never noticed the third sentence of the first
section of *Nothing Personal*. Baldwin begins
this section by laying bare the consequences
of living in a society so overdetermined by
consumerism. He opens with the image of
channel surfing (I imagine him holding an old
remote control. A recently lit cigarette in one
hand, the other clicking the remote over and
over again). He describes commercials that

promise Americans all sorts of material things that will make our lives meaningful—things that keep us forever young and trap us in our illusions of the wonderful life. It's like reading Max Horkheimer and Theodor Adorno about the modern condition and the manipulative nature of the culture industry. Much of this happens in one, seemingly interminable sentence. With dashes and semi-colons Baldwin relentlessly describes what America puts on offer and how we drown in it all. Here, ironically I suppose, he echoes Walt Whitman's "The Million Dead, Too, Summ'd Up"—one long sentence about our dead—as he accounts for the death of the American heart.

The long sentence mimics the onslaught of never-ending commercials that affirm the fantasy of American strength and prowess, a fantasy that leaves those of us who bear the brunt of its nonsense, here and abroad, in a state of despair and wonder. (Toni Morrison's character in *Beloved*, Stamp Paid, comes to mind: "What are these people?" he asked.) This powerful nation cleaves to myths about itself to evade what Baldwin describes as its "unspeakable loneliness." Here the modern condition as evidenced in those ghastly commercials takes on a particular kind of resonance—especially in the Jim Crow South. White Americans, within an "iron cage," are shackled to a mythical past that blocks them from confronting who they actually are. And this is a key insight for Baldwin, one he takes from *The Fire Next Time* and rewrites for *Nothing Personal*: "To be locked in the past means, in effect, that one has no past, since one can never assess it, or use it: and if one cannot use the past, one cannot function in the present, and so one can never be free. I take this to be . . . the American situation in relief, *the root of our unadmitted sorrow. . . .*" These particular people are trapped in a history they refused to know but carry within them. The terrors and panic they experience have everything to do with the gap between who they imagine themselves to be and who, deep down, they really are. That the nation actively evades confronting this gap locks the country into a kind of perpetual adolescence where those who desperately hold on to the American myth as some kind of new world

Eden refuse to grow up. And, for Baldwin, condemnation to eternal youth is "a synonym for corruption." Imagine being stuck forever in "Never, Never Land."

I can't help but connect this insight to what I witnessed over the four years of Donald Trump's presidency. Americans who refused to grow up reveled in the fantasy that Trump represented: that ours would remain a white nation in the vein of old Europe. All along it felt like a suppressed terror and panic lurked beneath the surface of their rants and hatreds—that the seams would unravel and reveal the true monstrosity hidden underneath a cheap-ass MAGA hat and T-shirt.

Baldwin opens *Nothing Personal* then with an extended riff on modern alienation in the context of the unique madness of the United States, a form of madness that still has a claim on us. Here the cold rationalization of modernity with its loss of genuine human intimacy combined with an unwavering faith in money and an unflinching commitment to white supremacy. All of which made the people who furiously walked the streets of this country, avoiding the eyes of those right in front of their faces, vapid and desperately lonely. In the place where dreams supposedly come true, Baldwin seemed to suggest that true joy was both fleeting and fugitive, and this made America a particularly nasty and sad place.

Who and what we have become as individuals in this country, tethered to a past filled with "niggers" and the white people who so desperately needed them, shape the substance of our living together as well as the self-understanding of the nation, which in turn shapes our individual identities. This hermeneutical circle (as that tortuous sentence reveals) amounts to a distinctive form of hell. Americans, Baldwin wrote, "are afraid to reveal ourselves because we trust ourselves so little." We lie about our virtue. We lie about our history to conceal our torment. In effect, Baldwin declared, "we live by lies." And those lies extend beyond matters of race and cut to the heart of our self-conception. Baldwin understood that our problems in the United States went beyond politics or the latest example of American racism. In a post-Trump world, we will soon see that he was not our only problem—just another indication of a more deep-seated American malaise.

Baldwin wrote of the lies that take root in the "secret chambers of our hearts":

> Nothing more sinister can happen, in any society, to any people. And when it happens, it means that the people are caught in a kind of vacuum between their present and their past—the romanticized, that is, the maligned past, and the denied and dishonored present. It is a crisis of identity. And in such a crisis, at such a pressure, it becomes absolutely indispensable to discover, or invent . . . the stranger, the barbarian, who is responsible for our confusion and our pain. Once

he is driven out—destroyed—then we can be at peace: those questions will be gone. Of course, those questions never go, but it has always seemed much easier to murder than to change. And this is really the choice with which we are confronted now.

The country needs its "niggers," its Islamic "terrorists," its "illegal aliens" to hold together a fragile identity that always seems to be on the verge of falling apart. The dangers, on this view, lie without and not within. (But Baldwin had already written in 1962 in an essay for the *New York Times Book Review*, after saying that the loneliness Dos Passos wrote about is now greater than ever before, that "the trouble is deeper than we wished to think: the trouble is in us.") If I am reading *Nothing Personal* correctly, the country needs its "strangers" to resolve the sense of alienation that threatens to suffocate this place. The enemy and evil without, and the violence we exact upon the threat they present or directly upon them, keeps us whole while the rot within corrupts everything.

Nothing Personal exposes all of this without a hint of sentimentality: that our failure to trust others, and more importantly, ourselves makes us mysteries to one another. Our greed and insatiable desire to hold on to what we have makes us susceptible to the lies; in fact, we become apostles of lies that justify the evils that make our way of life possible.

All of which makes love, genuine love, damn near impossible here. As Baldwin put it, "This is no place for love." He echoed this sentiment in *No Name in the Street* (1972): "I have always been struck, in America, by an emotional poverty so bottomless, and a terror of human life, of human touch, so deep, that virtually no American appears able to achieve any viable, organic connection between his public stance and his private life. This is what makes them so baffling, so moving, so exasperating, and so untrustworthy." Here we are today, even after the Trump presidency, and much remains the same.

In this essay, Baldwin exposes what motivates our nightly terrors. There is an emptiness here, and no amount of material possessions can fill it. There is an emptiness in us. And if we are to get at the root of white supremacy's hold on our lives, we will have to confront that emptiness directly, without the security of our legends. For Baldwin, this is no abstract matter, and one sees this at the end of *Nothing Personal*. Baldwin reveals his own torment— the desperation felt in the four a.m. hour that leads to a version of the question William James asked himself in 1895, "Is life worth living?" He knew, in his bones, that the specter of death, in the full light of our own failures and inadequacies, shadows our living and that our only recourse is the love of another human being.

The irony, of course, is that this must happen in such a loveless place. Baldwin has already said that America is not a place for love, but those words reflect the license of an artist. He knows love saved him, even though he never really believed that anyone could actually love him. And it is in this contrast that his faith in us is expressed: that in this country which refuses to grow up—that longs to be "the ageless American boy" and seeks refuge from responsibility in titillating and fleeting pleasures that offer the illusion of safety—we will one day "evolve into the knowledge that human beings are more important than real estate and will permit this knowledge to become the ruling principle of our lives."

While in Puerto Rico on vacation with his lover, Lucien Happersberger, Baldwin heard the news of the assassination of Medgar Evers, and he began writing *Nothing Personal* under the shadow of that death. Baldwin's family would later join him on the island—even his mother, Berdis, who did not like to fly, came. Among the many joys experienced, the family sat and read parts of Baldwin's new play, *Blues for Mister Charlie*. Between death and love, Baldwin found a way. *Nothing Personal* is a eulogy of sorts and a declaration of the will.

In the end, the power of love, of loving someone and of being loved, equips us to endure the world as it is and to imagine the world as it could be. Even the emptiness of America can be overcome, Baldwin maintained. We have the litany of the saints to bear witness to such a fact. They are those who through the horror and brutality of American life still loved and refused to die. William James answered the question "Is life worth living?" by asserting the power of belief: if you believe life is worth living, that belief will help create the fact. Baldwin finds no comfort in such abstractions, especially at four o'clock in the morning, when despair has one by the throat. Instead, the answer is found in the love of others who brought us through the storming sea—a kind of love that can break the sickness at the heart of America's darkness.

—Eddie S. Glaude Jr.

ABOUT
THE AUTHOR

J AMES BALDWIN was an American essayist, novelist, poet, and playwright whose eloquence and passion on the subjects of race, sexuality, and social justice in America made him an important voice in the US and, over his lifetime, through much of western Europe and into Asia.

The eldest of nine children, he was born in 1924 in New York and grew up in the Black ghetto of Harlem. As a young teen, he became active as a preacher in a small revivalist church, following in his stepfather's footsteps, a period he wrote about in his semiautobiographical first novel, *Go Tell It on the Mountain* (1953) and in his play about a woman evangelist, *The Amen Corner* (performed in New York City in 1965), as well as in his later novel *Just Above My Head*.

After graduation from high school, he moved to Greenwich Village, the "bohemian quarter" of New York City, where he subsisted through low-wage jobs and enriched himself with a study of literature. Feeling restless and unwelcome in his own country, he left in 1948 for Paris, where he lived for the next eight years. In later years, beginning in 1969, he became a "transatlantic commuter," living alternately in the south of France, in Istanbul, and in New York. His second novel, *Giovanni's Room* (1956), concerns an American in Paris torn between his love for a man and his love for a woman. The *New York Times* lauded the book as marked by an "unusual candor and yet with such dignity and intensity." Between the two novels came a landmark collection of essays, *Notes of a Native Son*, published by Beacon Press in 1955, which established Baldwin's importance as a sharp, deeply perceptive, and remarkably prescient social critic.

In 1957, he returned to the United States and became an active participant in the civil rights struggle that swept the nation. He began what would become a series of travels through the Southern states to document the struggles of the Black communities in real time.

His second book of essays, *Nobody Knows My Name* (1961), explores Black-white relations throughout the United States. This theme also was central to his novel *Another Country* (1962), which continues his deep dive into sexual identity as well as racial politics.

The *New Yorker* magazine gave over almost all of its November 17, 1962, issue to a long article by Baldwin on the Black Muslim separatist movement and other aspects of the civil rights struggle. The article became a best seller in book form as *The Fire Next Time* (1963). His searing play about racist oppression, *Blues for Mister Charlie*, had a Broadway run in 1964.

Baldwin continued to write important works in both fiction and nonfiction over the next decades, publishing a half dozen new books, including a collaboration with his high school friend, the photographer Richard Avedon, called *Nothing Personal*, which appeared as an oversized art book and was reprinted several times, though the title essay did not appear on its own until the Beacon Press edition of 2021. He also continued to write searingly honest fiction like *Going to Meet the Man* (1965), a collection of short stories; the novels *Tell Me How Long the Train's Been Gone* (1968), *If Beale Street Could Talk* (1974), and *Just Above My Head* (1979). In 1985, he turned back to his beloved genre of the essay and created a large collection of most of his nonfiction, *The Price of the Ticket* (1948–1985). Some issues of copyright prevented that important volume from staying in print or appearing in paperback until 2021. His last book was his first collection of poetry, *Jimmy's Blues*, reissued with a group of previously unpublished poems by Beacon Press in 2014.

Baldwin received numerous awards and was much sought after as a speaker, an activist, and a commentator until his untimely death, in 1987, in Saint Paul de Vence in the southeast of France.

For more about James Baldwin's life and work, please see *James Baldwin: A Biography*, by David Leeming, and *Begin Again: James Baldwin's America and Its Urgent Lessons for Our Own*, by Eddie S. Glaude Jr.

ABOUT THE
CONTRIBUTORS

ABOUT
IMANI PERRY

IMANI PERRY is the Hughes-Rogers Professor of African American Studies at Princeton University and a faculty associate with the
Programs in Law and Public Affairs, Gender
and Sexuality Studies, and Jazz Studies. She
is the author of six books, including *Breathe:
A Letter to My Sons*, which was a finalist for the
prestigious NAACP Image Award for Excel-
lence in Nonfiction and a finalist for the 2020

Chautauqua Prize, and *Looking for Lorraine: The Radiant and Radical Life of Lorraine Hansberry*, which received the Pen Bograd-Weld Award for Biography, the Phi Beta Kappa Christian Gauss Award for outstanding work in literary scholarship, the Lambda Literary Award for LGBTQ Nonfiction, and the Shilts-Grahn Award for nonfiction from the Publishing Triangle. Her book *May We Forever Stand: A History of the Black National Anthem*, was the winner of the 2019 American Studies Association's John Hope Franklin Book Award for the best book in American studies and the Hurston/Wright Award for Nonfiction and a finalist for an NAACP Image Award. Her most recent book is *South to America: A Journey Below the Mason Dixon to Understand the Soul of a Nation*.

Perry is a scholar of law and of literary and cultural studies, and an author of creative nonfiction. She earned her PhD in American studies from Harvard University, a JD from Harvard Law School, an LLM from Georgetown University Law Center, and a BA in literature and American studies from Yale College. Her writing and scholarship primarily focuses on the history of Black thought, art, and imagination crafted in response to, and resistance against, the social, political, and legal realities of domination in the West. She lives outside Philadelphia with her two sons, Freeman Diallo Perry Rabb and Issa Garner Rabb.

ABOUT
EDDIE S. GLAUDE JR.

EDDIE S. GLAUDE JR. is the James S. Mc-Donnell Distinguished University Professor and chair of the Department of African American Studies at Princeton University, a program he first became involved with shaping as a doctoral candidate in religion at Princeton. Among his well-known books are *Democracy in Black: How Race Still Enslaves the American Soul* and *In a Shade of Blue: Pragmatism and the Politics of Black America*, both of which take a wide look at black communities, the difficulties of race in the United States, and the challenges our democracy face.

He took his undergraduate degree from Morehouse College, where he was elected the student-body president, and he holds a master's degree in African American studies from Temple University and both an MA and a PhD in religion from Princeton University. He is a columnist for *Time* magazine and an MSNBC contributor on many of their programs. He also regularly appears on NBC TV's *Meet the Press*. Glaude hosts the podcast *AAS 21*, recorded at Princeton University in Stanhope Hall, the African American Studies Department's home. He is the recipient of numerous awards, including the Carl A. Fields Award and the Modern Language Association's William Sanders Scarborough Book Prize and has been a visiting scholar in African American studies at Harvard University and Amherst College.

His most recent book is the highly acclaimed *Begin Again: James Baldwin's America and Its Urgent Lessons for Our Own*, which Edwidge Danticat aptly described as "filled with the type of passion, lyricism, and fire that James Baldwin commands and deserves. . . . This phenomenal work [is] a timeless and spellbinding conversation between two brilliant writers."